P9-CRP-888

CHRISTMAS SCROLL SAW PATTERNS

CHRISTMAS SCROLL SAW PATTERNS

Patrick & Patricia Spielman

Sterling Publishing Co., Inc. New York

Library of Congress Cataloging-in-Publication Data

Spielman, Patrick E.
    Christmas scroll saw patterns / by Patrick and Patricia Spielman.
      p. cm.
    "Essentially an extension of our . . . Scroll saw holiday patterns
    (Sterling Publishing, 1991)"—Introd.
    Includes index.
    ISBN 0-8069-0308-2
    1. Jig saws. 2. Woodwork. 3. Christmas decorations.
  I. Spielman, Patricia. II. Spielman, Patrick E. Scroll saw holiday
patterns. III. Title.
TT186.S6678   1993
745.594'12—dc20   93–3417
                                    CIP

10 9 8 7 6 5

Published by Sterling Publishing Company, Inc.
387 Park Avenue South, New York, N.Y. 10016
© 1992 by Patrick and Patricia Spielman
Distributed in Canada by Sterling Publishing
℅ Canadian Manda Group, P.O. Box 920, Station U
Toronto, Ontario, Canada M8Z 5P9
Distributed in Great Britain and Europe by Cassell PLC
Villiers House, 41/47 Strand, London WC2N 5JE, England
Distributed in Australia by Capricorn Link Ltd.
P.O. Box 665, Lane Cove, NSW 2066
Manufactured in the United States of America
All rights reserved

Sterling ISBN 0–8069–0308–2

Contents

Color section follows page 64.

Metric Conversion

INCHES TO MILLIMETRES AND CENTIMETRES

MM—millimetres　　*CM—centimetres*

Inches	MM	CM	Inches	CM	Inches	CM
⅛	3	0.3	9	22.9	30	76.2
¼	6	0.6	10	25.4	31	78.7
⅜	10	1.0	11	27.9	32	81.3
½	13	1.3	12	30.5	33	83.8
⅝	16	1.6	13	33.0	34	86.4
¾	19	1.9	14	35.6	35	88.9
⅞	22	2.2	15	38.1	36	91.4
1	25	2.5	16	40.6	37	94.0
1¼	32	3.2	17	43.2	38	96.5
1½	38	3.8	18	45.7	39	99.1
1¾	44	4.4	19	48.3	40	101.6
2	51	5.1	20	50.8	41	104.1
2½	64	6.4	21	53.3	42	106.7
3	76	7.6	22	55.9	43	109.2
3½	89	8.9	23	58.4	44	111.8
4	102	10.2	24	61.0	45	114.3
4½	114	11.4	25	63.5	46	116.8
5	127	12.7	26	66.0	47	119.4
6	152	15.2	27	68.6	48	121.9
7	178	17.8	28	71.1	49	124.5
8	203	20.3	29	73.7	50	127.0

About the Authors

Patrick Spielman's love of wood began when, as a child, he transformed fruit crates into toys. Now this prolific and innovative woodworker is respected worldwide as a teacher and author.

His most famous contribution to the woodworking field has been his perfection of a method to season green wood with polyethylene glycol 1000 (PEG). He went on to invent, manufacture, and distribute the PEG-Thermovat chemical seasoning system.

During his many years as shop instructor in Wisconsin, Mr. Spielman published manuals, teaching guides, and more than 40 popular books, including *Modern Wood Technology*, a college text. He also wrote six educational series on wood technology, tool use, processing techniques, design, and wood-product planning.

Author of the best-selling *Router Handbook*, Mr. Spielman has served as editorial consultant to a professional magazine and as advisor and consultant to power tool manufacturers, and his products, techniques, and many books have been featured in numerous periodicals and on national television.

This pioneer of new ideas and inventor of countless jigs, fixtures, and designs used throughout the world is a unique combination of expert woodworker and brilliant teacher—all of which have endeared him to his many readers and to his publisher.

Patricia Spielman (Mrs. Pat) has co-authored three other books with her husband, Patrick, including their first and best-selling *Scroll Saw Pattern Book*. As both a buyer of wood products and the creator of Spielmans WoodWorks Gift Shop and Gallery, Mrs. Pat plays an invaluable role in the overall operations of the varied and well-known Spielmans WoodWorks businesses. Recently Mrs. Pat and daughter, Sherri Valitchka, opened a new gift gallery, Spielmans Kid Works, which features high-quality wood toys and furniture. Mrs. Pat is highly respected locally and nationally for her discerning eye for design and her natural artistic abilities, all of which are evident not only in the Spielmans' books, but also in their trend-setting WoodWorks Gallery.

Should you wish to contact the Spielmans, please send your correspondence to Sterling Publishing Company.

Acknowledgment

We thank our daughters, Sherri and Sandy, for their valuable help. The shading on many of the pattern designs, making them easier to use, is the result of Sherri's efforts and the assistance of Jenny Blahnik. Thanks to Sandy for contributing original patterns, retouching photos, and assisting with project painting. We thank Edward Toby for the design concept utilized to develop the unusual Christmas tree project on page 141. A hearty thanks goes to Dirk Boelman's Art Factory for doing the great tracings of the finished art, and a big thank you once again to the multitalented Julie Kiehnau, our expert scroll-sawyer and typist, for her excellent work in both areas.

Illus. 1. This book provides enough ornament patterns to entirely decorate your Christmas tree.

Introduction

Christmas Scroll Saw Patterns is essentially an extension of our previous and very popular book, *Scroll Saw Holiday Patterns* (Sterling Publishing, 1991), of which a major part is devoted to Christmas designs. The demand for Christmas patterns has continued, because Christmas is the longest and most important of all seasons for the do-it-yourselfer. *Christmas Scroll Saw Patterns* has been prepared for those scroll sawing woodworkers who become captivated by the spirit of the season.

Should you, for example, want to decorate your entire Christmas tree with ornaments (Illus. 1) that showcase your sawing talents, you will find plenty of patterns here. The same tree-ornament designs can be used to decorate your home in a variety of other ways. Hang them in your windows as light-catchers (see Illus. 2 and 3), or wherever it seems appropriate—on mirrors and walls, for example.

Illus. 2. Decorate windows and mirrors with hanging ornaments. Here, a collection of cutouts is combined with hanging ornaments to decorate the kitchen.

Illus. 3. Small suction cups, available from most variety stores, permit you to hang ornaments anywhere.

Stacking layers of thin solid wood or layers of very thin plywood together and cutting them all at once produces many ornaments in just slightly more time than it takes to cut one. Illus. 4 shows ornaments that can also be used as unusual tags on wrapped gifts; leave the wood unfinished and write your message with a waterproof pen.

Giving neighbors, friends, and relatives your scroll sawn handiwork is always a welcome gesture. If the giving mood strikes heavily, make Christmas objects for church bazaars and other charities. Handmade ornaments make ideal gifts for your favorite teachers, for the mailman, etc. A hand-sawn ornament makes a personal and memorable hostess gift during the festive holiday season.

Likewise, any scroll saw Christmas project makes a good gift not only to others, but to yourself too (see Illus. 5, 6, and 7). Some patterns are a bit more detailed than others and take longer to make, but basic scroll saw techniques may be used for almost all the patterns in this book. If scroll sawing is new for you, we recommend you read another of our books, *Scroll Saw Basics*, which provides essential instruction on scroll saws and how to use them to make basic cuts.

Illus. 4. Stack sawing ¹⁄₁₆"-thick plywood is the easiest way to make many of these unusual gift tags.

Illus. 5. Another decorative window arrangement.

Illus. 6. The Mother and Child segmentation project is the focal point of a mantle decoration.

Illus. 7. Sleigh project as a table centerpiece. The sleigh can be packed with a variety of Christmas goodies.

Basic Techniques

Sizing, Copying, and Transferring Patterns

Christmas Scroll Saw Patterns contains many new designs and projects in ready-to-use patterns. Most of these patterns are presented in what we think are usable full sizes. However, because individual needs and preferences vary, we hope that you will change the sizes of our patterns or modify them to satisfy your particular needs. For example, small hanging ornaments may be enlarged to make huge lawn-size or yard-size decorations; conversely, some of our larger cutouts can be reduced to make small hanging ornaments. Experiment with several changes of size, as desired.

The easiest and fastest way to enlarge or reduce patterns is with the assistance of a modern office copying machine. If one is not available for your use, there are other methods and tools you can use that have traditionally been used for enlarging drawings, such as the square grid method and the pantographs.

A pattern enlarged on a copying machine is highly desirable, because it is accurate and it can be applied directly to the wood for a sawing guide (see Illus. 8). The copies can be temporarily bonded directly onto the surface of the wood, using a brush-on rubber cement or a temporary bonding spray adhesive (Illus. 9). We prefer the spray-adhesive technique. There are several spray adhesives available that will work, but we recommend a spray mount artist's adhesive such as 3M's Scotch brand. Most photography stores and studios carry this, as do art graphics and

Illus. 8. Any small scroll saw can be used to make most of the projects in this book. Here 1"-thick wood with a copied pattern applied to it is cut with a narrow blade.

craft supply stores. One can will last about a year. It's a great time-saving product.

To use the adhesive, simply spray a very light mist onto the back of the copied pattern—do not spray directly on the wood (see Illus. 9). Wait 10 to 30 seconds, press the pattern onto your wood (Illus. 10) with hand pressure, and presto! you're ready to begin sawing—just that easy and just that quick! Gone are the frustrations of doing tracings, working with messy carbon papers, and similar techniques that never really produced the clear, crisp, accurate layout lines that are so essential to good sawing.

Saw following the lines of the pattern. When sawing is completed, the pattern is easily peeled off the workpiece (Illus. 11). The adhesive leaves virtually no residue on the wood that might inhibit subsequent finishing. We recommend that you test the tack qualities of the adhesive to be sure that, at first use, you are spraying just enough for an effective temporary bond, and no more. Should the pattern be difficult to remove, simply wipe the top of the pattern with a rag slightly dampened in solvent.

If you decide to use the rubber-cement method to bond a machine-copied pattern

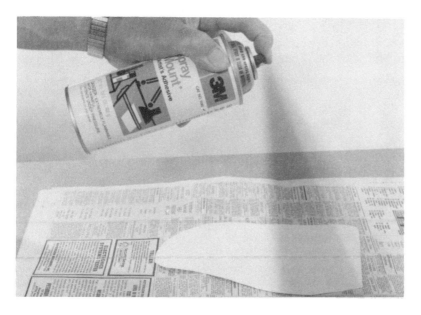

Illus. 9. Apply a very light mist of spray adhesive only to the back of the pattern. Do not spray directly onto the wood. Note that a newspaper underneath the pattern is being used to catch the overspray.

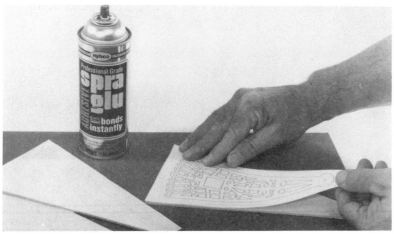

Illus. 10. Press down the spray-adhesive-coated copy of the pattern directly onto the wood workpiece blank.

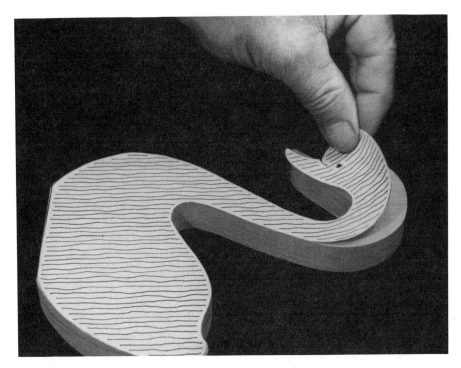

Illus. 11. After sawing is completed, the pattern lifts off the wood easily, leaving no residue to interfere with finishing.

to the workpiece, a little more care is required. Do not brush on too heavy a coat. If some cement remains on the wood you peel off the pattern, it can be removed by rubbing it off with your fingers. Do not use solvents applied directly to the wood.

Stack-Sawing Techniques

Stack-sawing involves layering one or more pieces of wood on top of another and sawing them all at once. This technique produces perfectly identical cut pieces and saves time. The layers can be held together in a variety of ways, such as nailing or gluing in the waste areas, using double-faced tape (use very little), wrapping around the stack with masking tape, or stapling the layers together through the waste along the edges. All of these will

work; however, certain patterns are better handled with one method than another. **Tip:** Use spray adhesive applied to both sides of a strip of paper to make your own double-faced tape. This trick works especially well when stack-sawing thin wood—wood too thin to nail or tack together.

Wood Materials

The patterns given here can be sawn from a wide variety of different materials and in a variety of different thicknesses—most of these choices are entirely yours. In some cases we specify or suggest suitable thicknesses where it's important to the visual impact or structural requirements of a particular design. Use cheap soft woods, as a practical choice, if the cutouts are to be coated with opaque finishes. Some of the more highly detailed, fretted designs may be best sawn from plywoods, which are more durable, but sometimes less attractive, than solid woods are.

Ways to Utilize Patterns

In addition to enlarging or reducing patterns to your own size preferences, there are several other ways to individualize patterns. Wall-hanging designs can be made into utility projects by adding pegs or hooks to hang various things on. Standing designs can be converted to door stops simply by nailing a thin wedge to the back side. Glue magnets on designs to make refrigerator-type note holders. Use designs as overlay decorations on boxes, clocks, signs, furniture, and various household accessories. Attach metal findings to the backs of small cutouts with epoxy glue to make jewelry. Add glued-on bows, lace, and pieces of fabric to give personality and color to otherwise bland cutouts. Gift tags or tree ornaments may be sawn of thin plywood.

Finishing Cutouts

There are lots of ways and different materials to finish your holiday cutout decorations and ornaments. Natural finishes, stains, and paints are all good; your choice is a matter of personal preference. Many patterns have lines on the "faces" of cutouts to give them some personality or character. Lines representing eyes, mouth, clothes, and the like can be painted or wood-burned, whatever is in line with your artistic inclinations.

Some patterns lend themselves well to segmentation (see Illus. 6), in which the pattern is cut apart into segments along the lines of the pattern that suggest certain expressive features. All sawn edges are rounded slightly using sandpaper pads or files, or a portable router for larger pieces. (See Santa wall plaque, pages 96–98, for further details of this process.)

The individual pieces or segments are put back together again prior to being stained or painted: glue the segments to each other or to a thin backing material to make the whole.

Illus 12. Tree ornaments made from a variety of ¼″-thick hardwoods.

Illus. 13. More tree ornaments made from ¼"-thick hardwood

Patterns

22

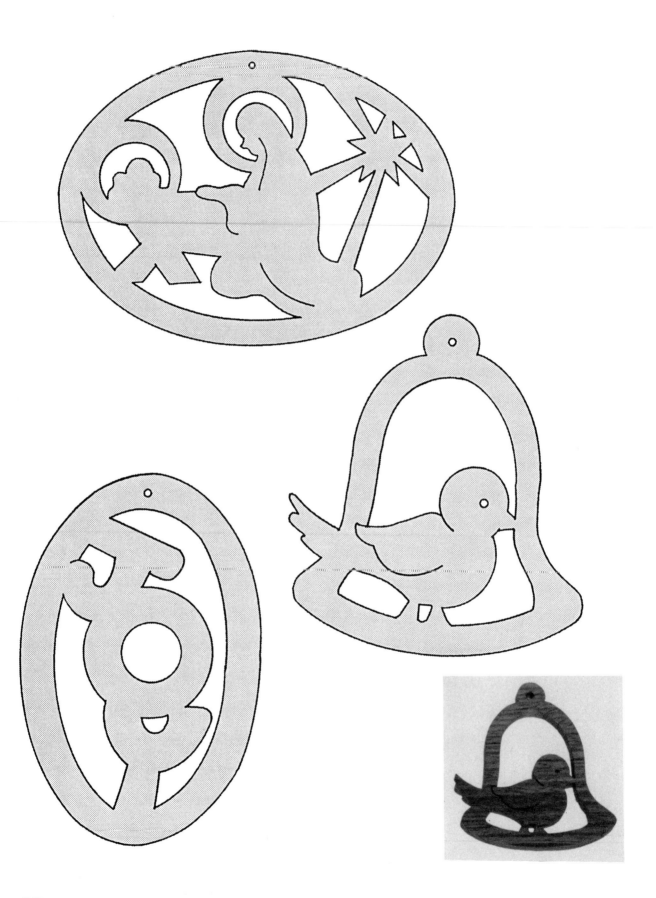

Illus. 14. Large cutout ornaments can be made from proportionally thicker material. The one on the right is cut from ⅜"-thick material; its outside edges were rounded over with a router.

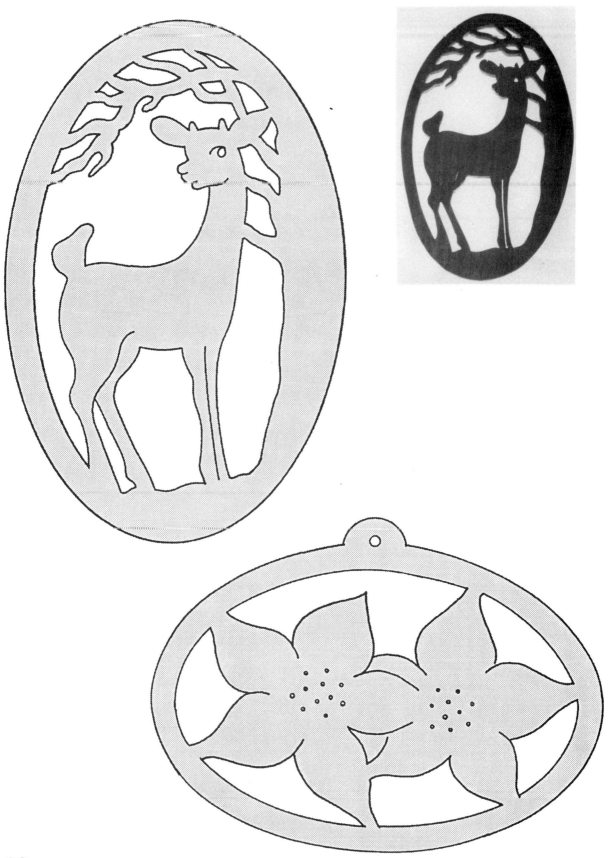

To:

From:

Illus. 15. Gift tags sawn of thin plywood can also be used as tree ornaments.

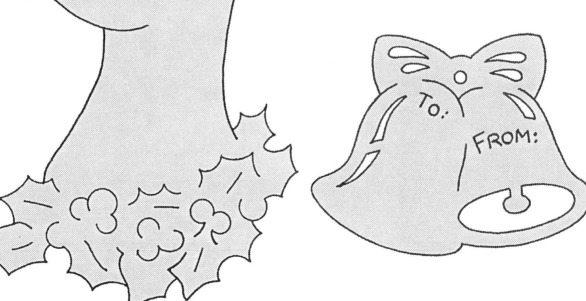

To:

From:

38

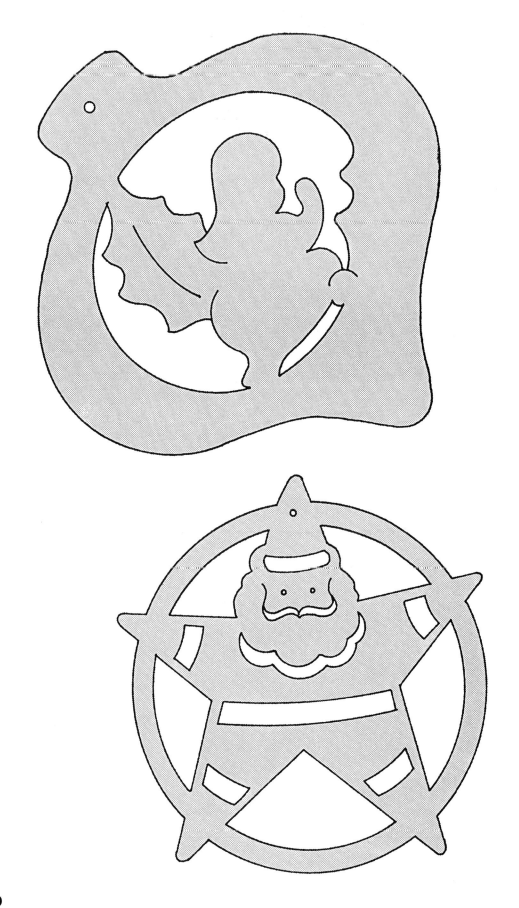

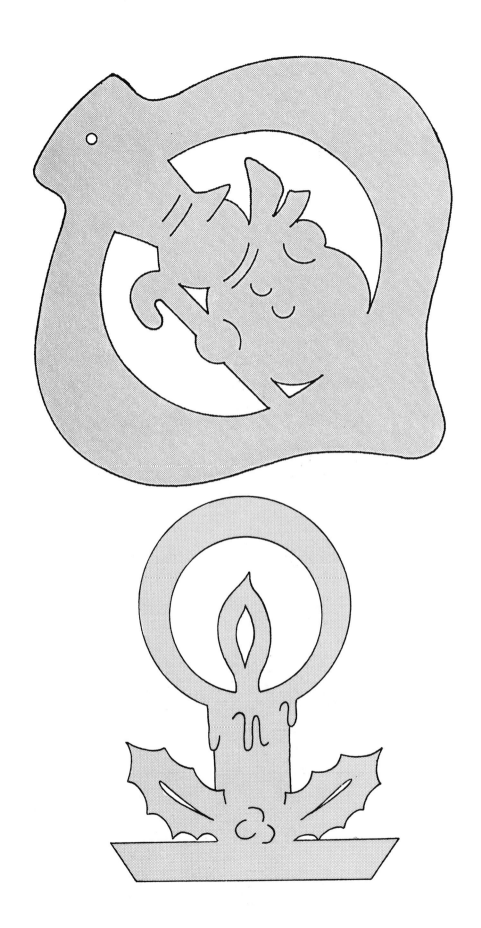

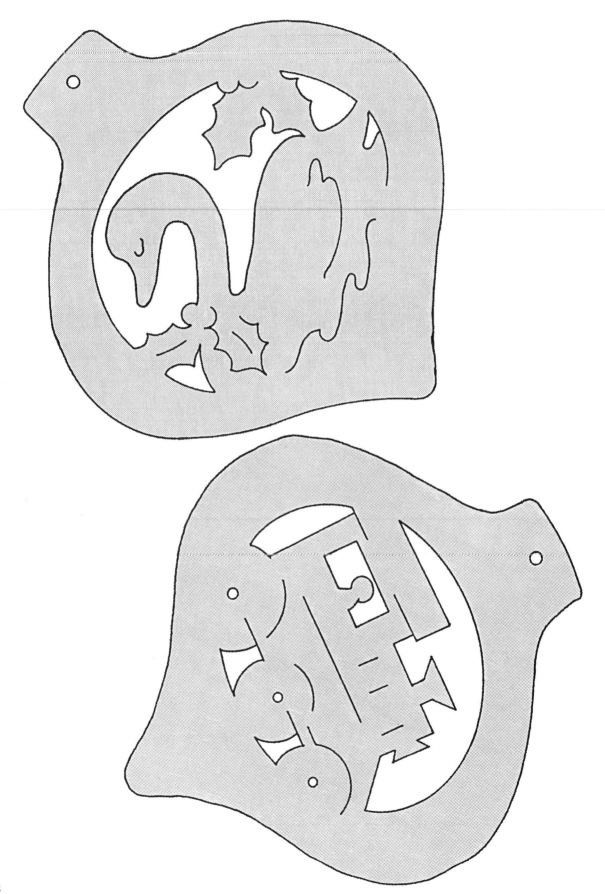

Wings are traced and cut separately and glued on.

Illus. 16. Painted cut-outs (patterns on page 48).

Pierced tree designs.

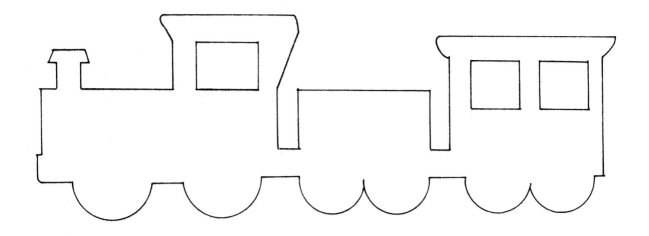

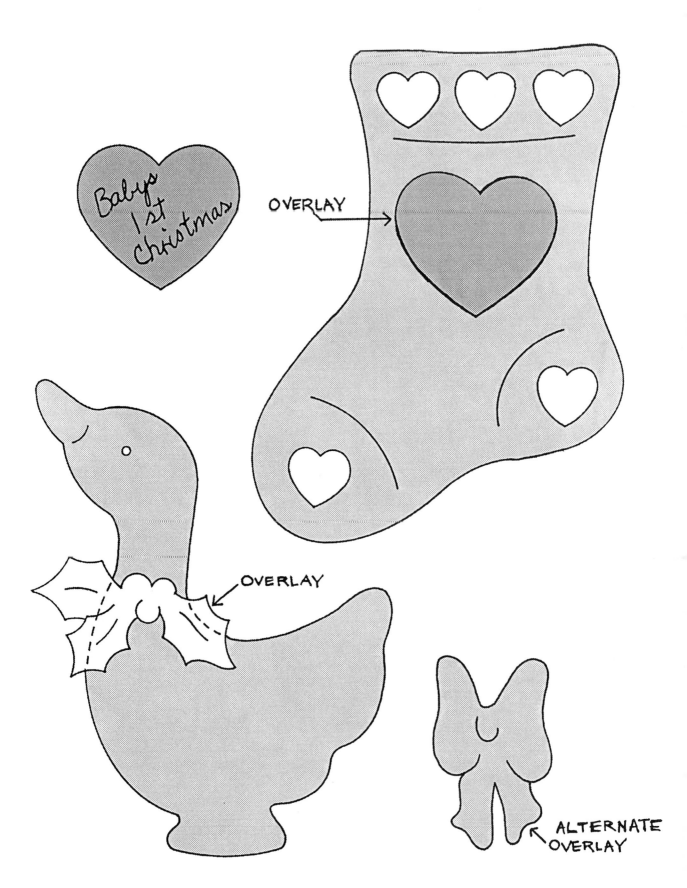

Baby's 1st Christmas

OVERLAY

OVERLAY

ALTERNATE OVERLAY

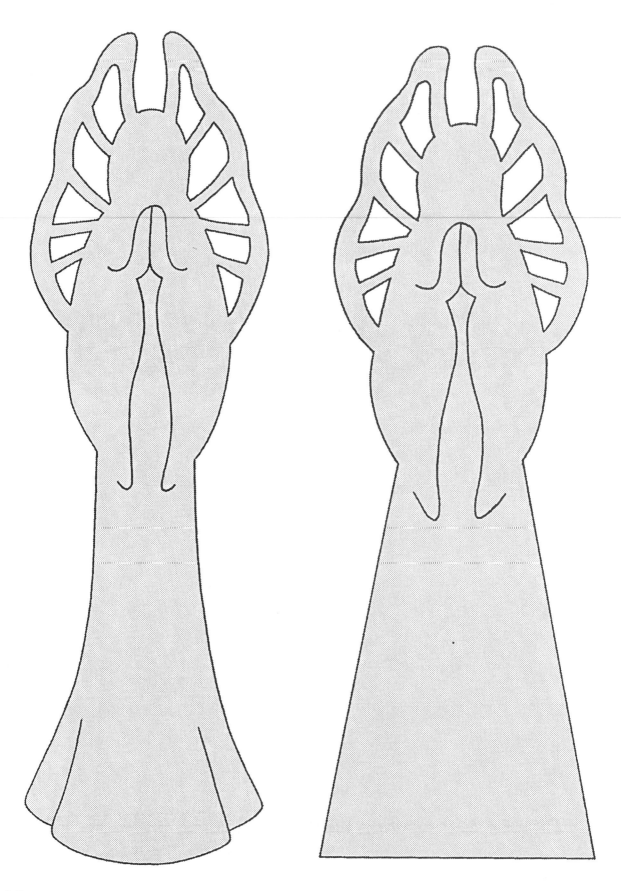

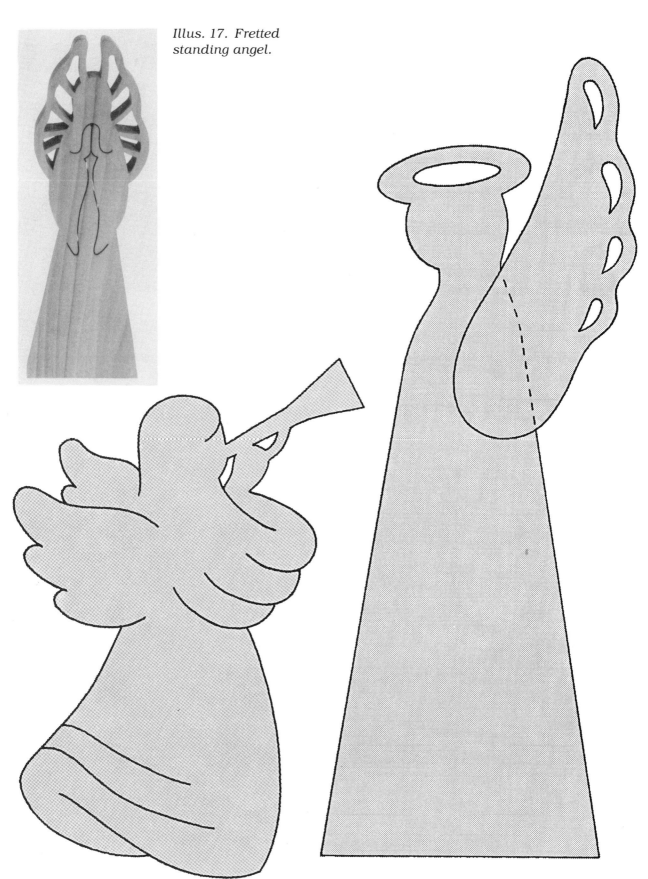

Illus. 17. Fretted standing angel.

Angels with tapers (p. 67); layered angels
(p. 66, 68), which are glued and painted.

Reindeer (p. 90–91); sleigh (p. 94–95); teddy
bear Santa (p. 83); standing Santa (p. 81).

Shelf with miniature cutouts (p. 120–122).

Segmented Santa (p. 98); segmented Mother and
Child (p. 100–101).

Christmas tree ornaments (p. 20, 22, 23, 24, 28, and 42). All were sawn from solid ¼-thick hardwoods.

Nativity (p. 118) cut from ¾"-thick prestained pine.

Teddy bear Santa (p. 83); solid trees (p. 138); rocking horse (p. 103).

Elves (p. 87–89); solid trees (p. 138).

Christmas tree ornaments (p. 24, 28, 32, 33, 36, 37).

Candle and holly (p. 116); napkin rings (p. 72).

"Merry Christmas" wreath (p. 110–111) cut from plywood; roly-poly cutouts (p. 48) sawn from ¼"-thick solid basswood.

Standing painted St. Nicholas (p. 85); NOEL sign (p. 146, 147).

Symmetrical reindeer heads (p. 70); snowflakes (p. 137); star-shaped Santa (p. 40); Nativity (p. 113); poinsettia (p. 132–133); deer in oval (p. 35).

Gift tags (p. 38, 39) sawn from thin plywood.

Fretted standing angel (p. 62); toy soldier (p. 107); seated teddy bear (p. 105); all were sawn from ¾"-thick wood.

"Joy" cut out and painted from Santa alphabet patterns (p. 148–154); trees with cutout centers (p. 51).

Illus. 18. Painted angel made of layered pieces.

Illus. 19. These angels should be cut from at least ¾″-thick material. Use birthday cake candles as decorations only. Do not burn these candles.

67

Illus. 20. Another painted angel made of layered parts.

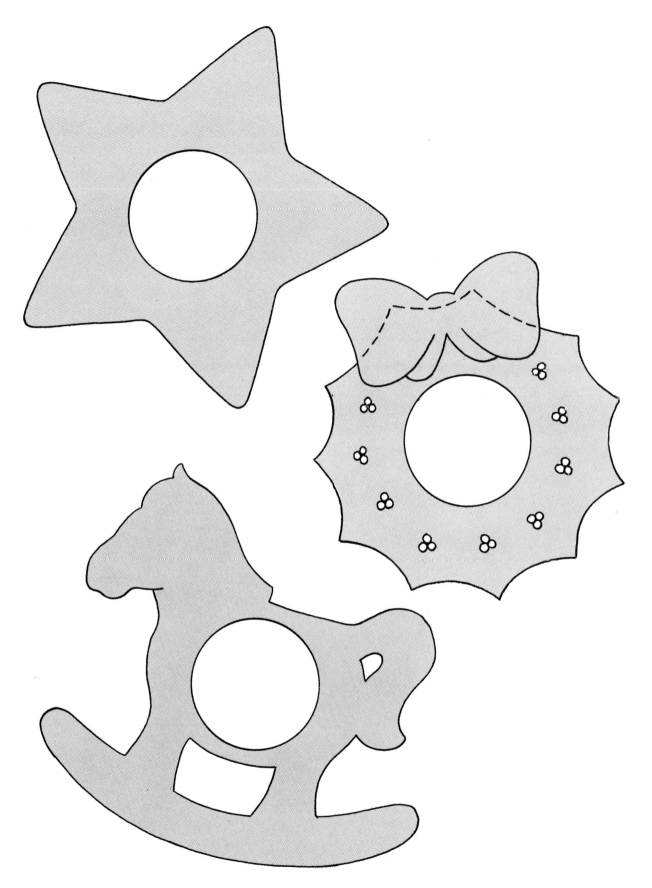

Illus. 21. Napkin rings cut from ¾" wood with some painted detailing.

Above: assembled reindeer and sleigh.
Below: reindeer pattern.

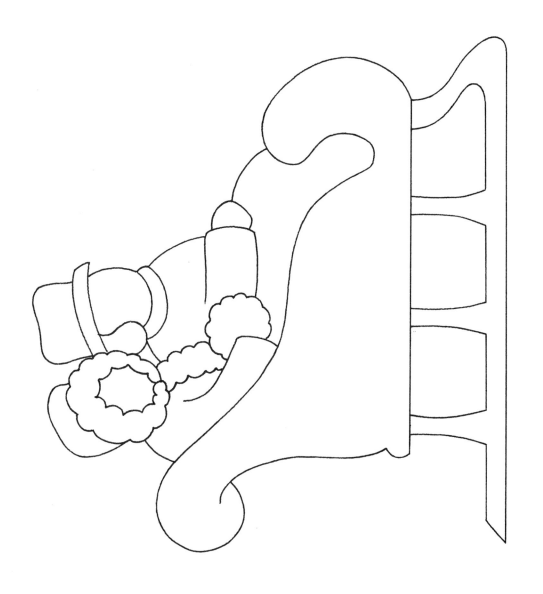

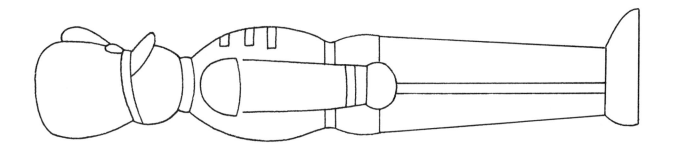

78

Illus. 22. Standing painted
Santa, cut from thick wood.

82

Illus. 23. Standing teddy bear Santa with painted details, cut from thick wood.

Illus. 24. Standing painted St. Nicks, cut from thick material (pattern on facing page).

86

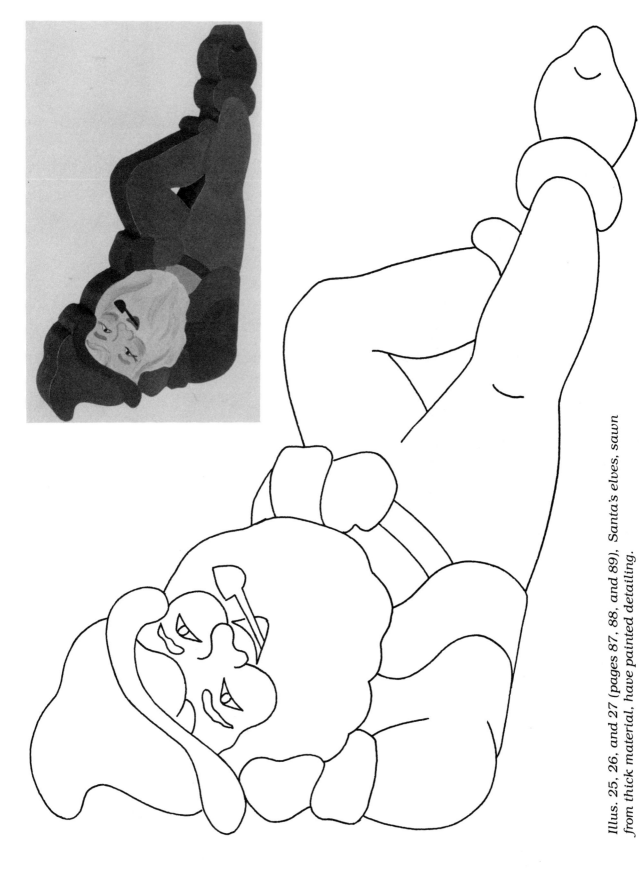

Illus. 25, 26, and 27 (pages 87, 88, and 89), Santa's elves, sawn from thick material, have painted detailing.

90

Illus. 28. Standing reindeer has
some painted details. Rounding of
the outside edges of the legs is
optional.

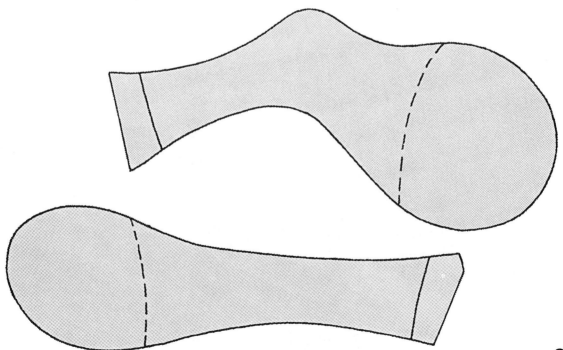

Illus. 29. Sleigh centerpiece features optional router-cut dado joinery and rounded edges. It is shown in two sizes. The large sleigh is double the size of the patterns given here.

Illus. 30. Optional dadoes for the front and back make for good construction and easier assembly. Cut dadoes to a depth equal to ⅓ of the stock thickness. If not using dado construction, the front and back patterns must be reduced accordingly in size: ¼" less for the small sleigh and ½" less in total size for the large sleigh.

Illus. 31. Rounding over the edges of the small sleigh's runners on a router table. Use a corner-rounding bit with a ⅛" or 3/16" radius on this and all other parts of the small-size sleigh.

Illus. 32. Rounding over the runners of the large-size sleigh with a hand-held router. Use a 5/16" or ⅜" radius corner-rounding bit.

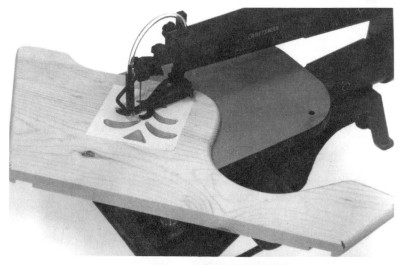

Illus. 33. Stop the round-over cuts short of the dadoes, as shown.

Illus. 34. Making the pierced tree design cuts using the scroll saw.

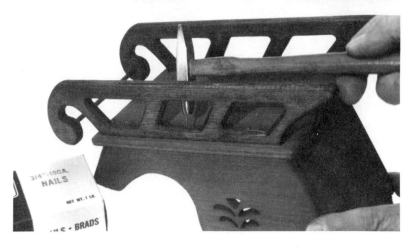

Illus. 35. Making a test assembly of the back and/or front to sides. Note: It's recommended you stain all pieces before final assembly.

Illus. 36. Nail the bottom of the sides and then mount the runners by toe-nailing from the inside, as shown.

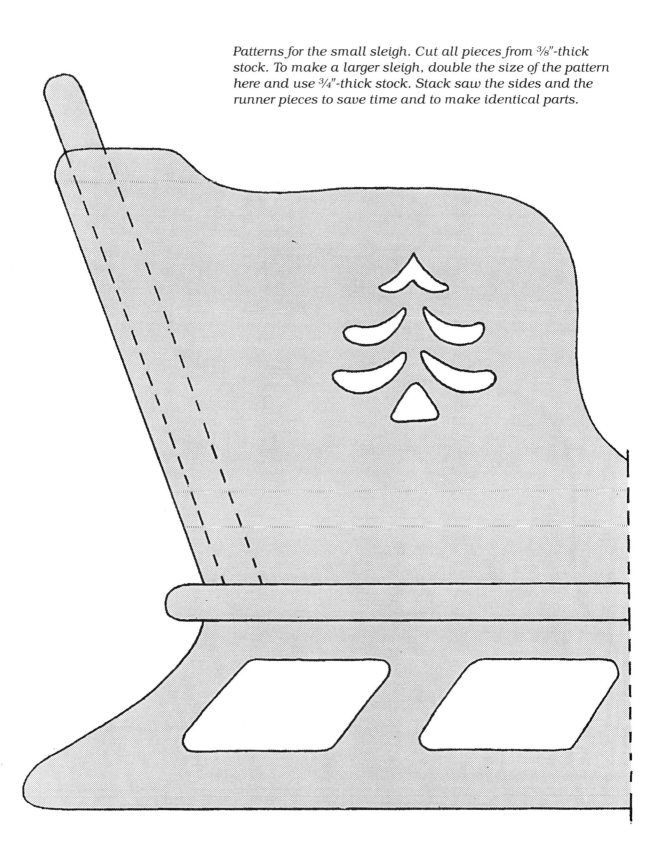

Patterns for the small sleigh. Cut all pieces from ⅜"-thick stock. To make a larger sleigh, double the size of the pattern here and use ¾"-thick stock. Stack saw the sides and the runner pieces to save time and to make identical parts.

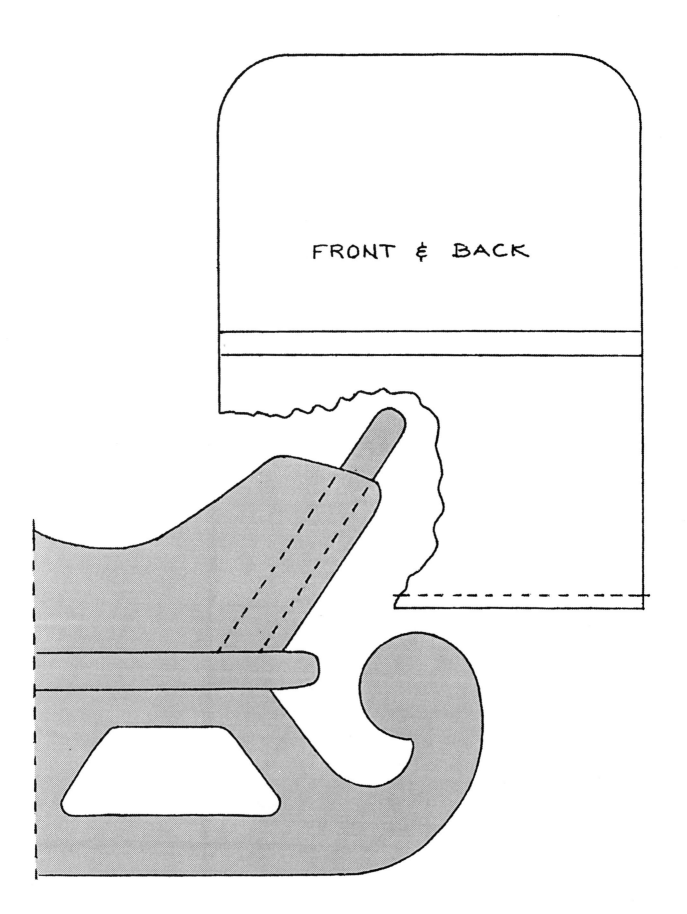

FRONT & BACK

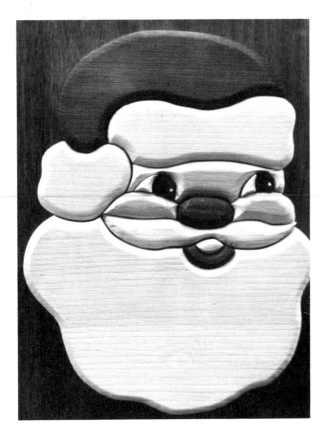

Illus. 37. Segmented Santa wall plaque. Cut the pattern into individual pieces, stain or paint each part, and reassemble by gluing them to a thin backing.

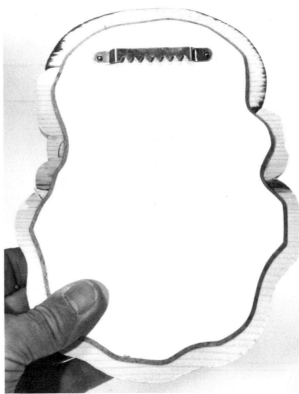

Illus. 38. Back view of the segmented Santa face. Note that the backing is sawn smaller than the face profile. The backing is also bevel-sawn at approximately 30–35 degrees.

Illus. 39. Scroll-sawing the various segments of the Santa face from ¾"-thick pine. It is best to orientate the pattern on the wood so the grain direction will be horizontal or in line with Santa's mustache.

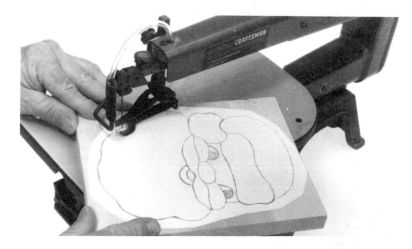

Illus. 40. Round the edges of the individual pieces by hand or by using special router techniques. Note the use of the router pad, which eliminates the need for clamping. Another piece helps to support the router, keeping it from tipping. The edges of the very small parts should be rounded by hand using a rasp or knife and sandpaper.

Illus. 41. A ¼"-radius corner-rounding bit and the router setup for rounding over small parts. This custom sub-base made of clear plastic (or plywood) with zero clearance around the bit replaces the factory sub-base.

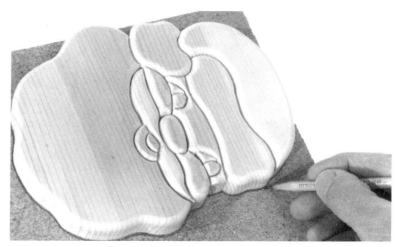

Illus. 42. Preparing the backing. The actual backing is cut about ¼" to ⅜" smaller than the initial outline marked out here. Once the base is cut, the individual parts are glued onto it, after each piece is stained or painted.

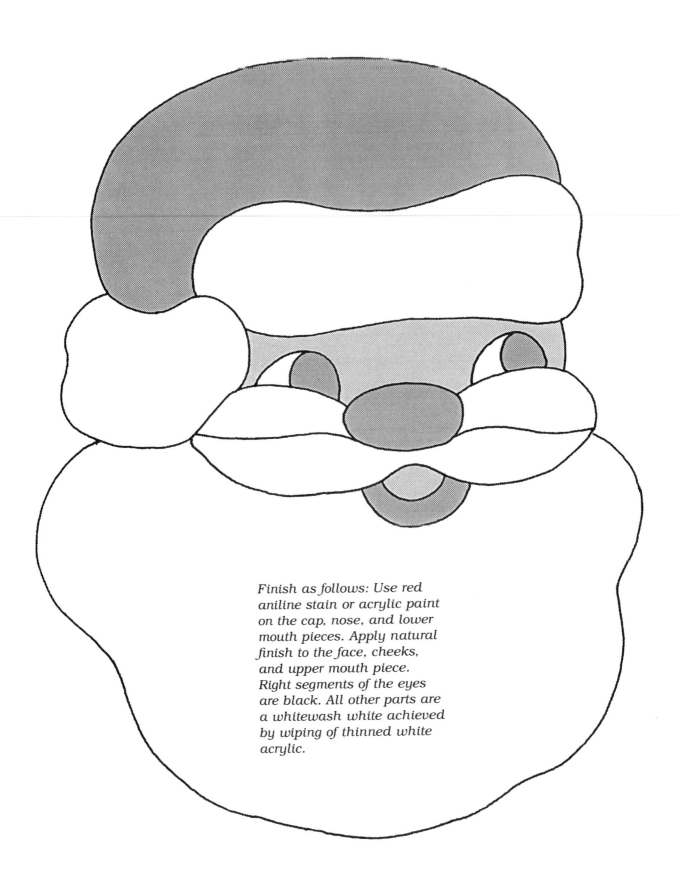

Finish as follows: Use red aniline stain or acrylic paint on the cap, nose, and lower mouth pieces. Apply natural finish to the face, cheeks, and upper mouth piece. Right segments of the eyes are black. All other parts are a whitewash white achieved by wiping of thinned white acrylic.

98

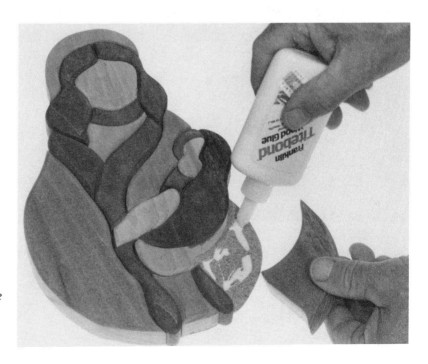

Illus. 43. Mother and Child segmentation project. In this project, stains in natural, medium and dark intensities provide the coloring.

Illus. 44. Do not stain the backs or inside edges of the pieces. Here the prestained parts are glued to a thin backing material.

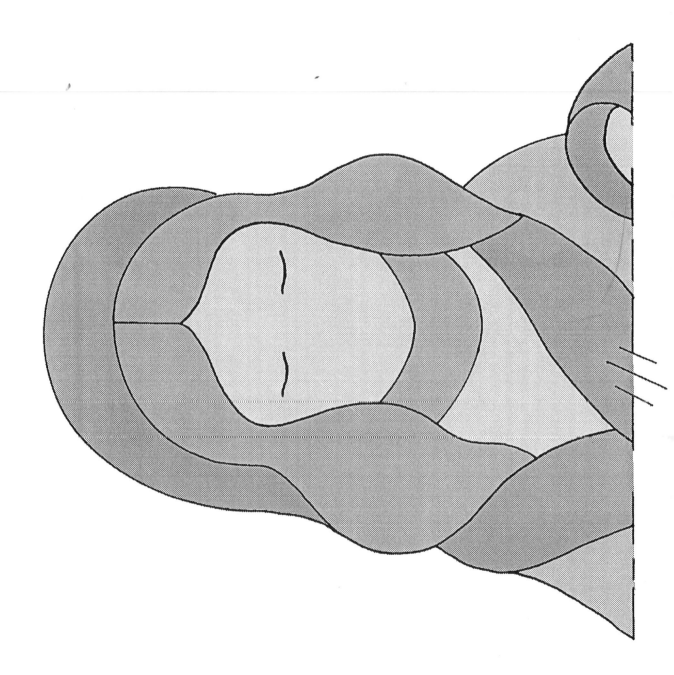

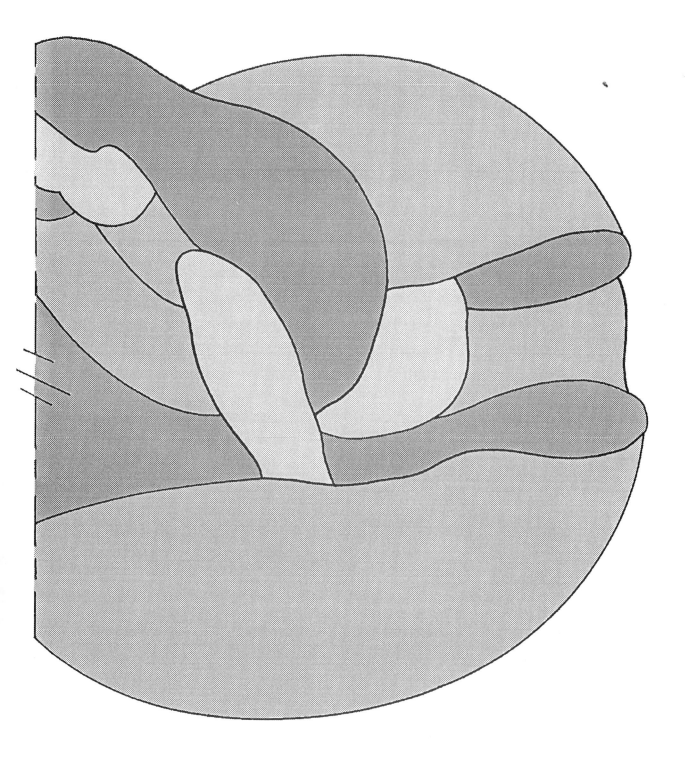

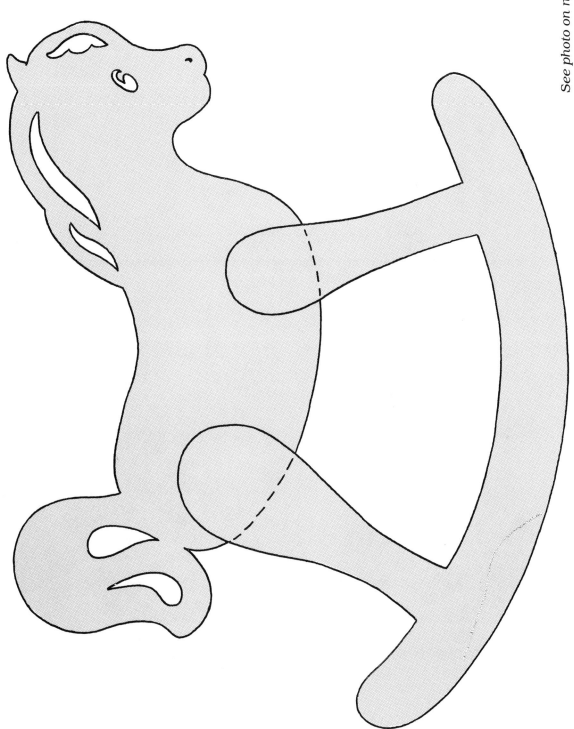

See photo on next page.

Illus. 45. Small decorative rocking horse has body and leg rockers cut from ¾″-thick wood.

Illus. 46. Christmas teddy bear.

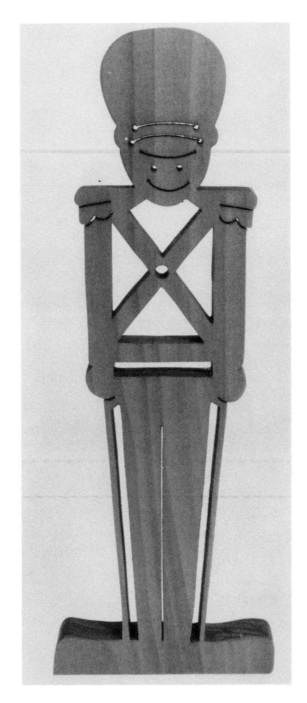

Illus. 47. This standing toy soldier can be made in various sizes, but the material should have sufficient thickness to stand alone.

Illus. 48. This Christmas message is best made from plywood. Pattern on pages 110 and 111.

A

B

110

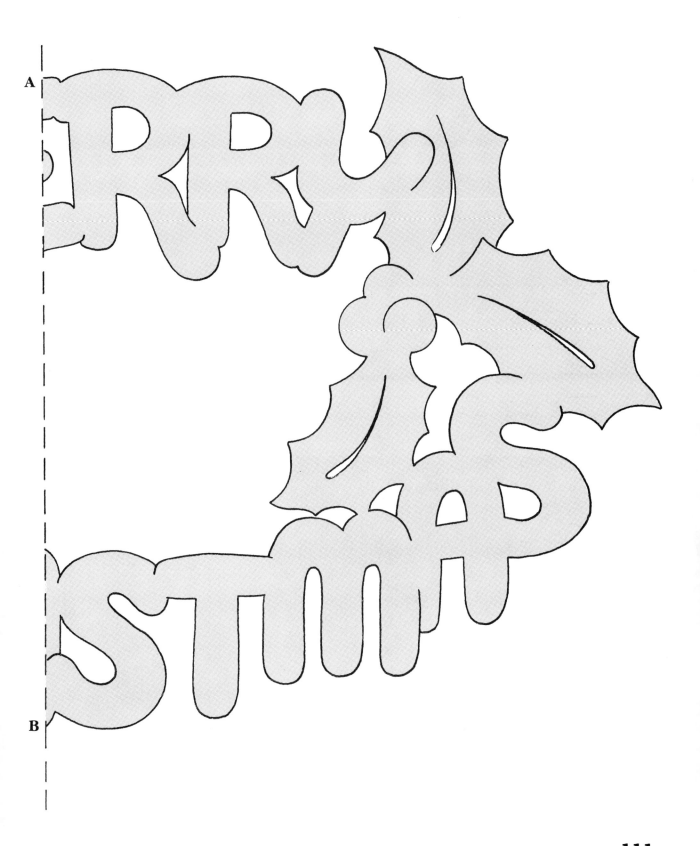

A

B

111

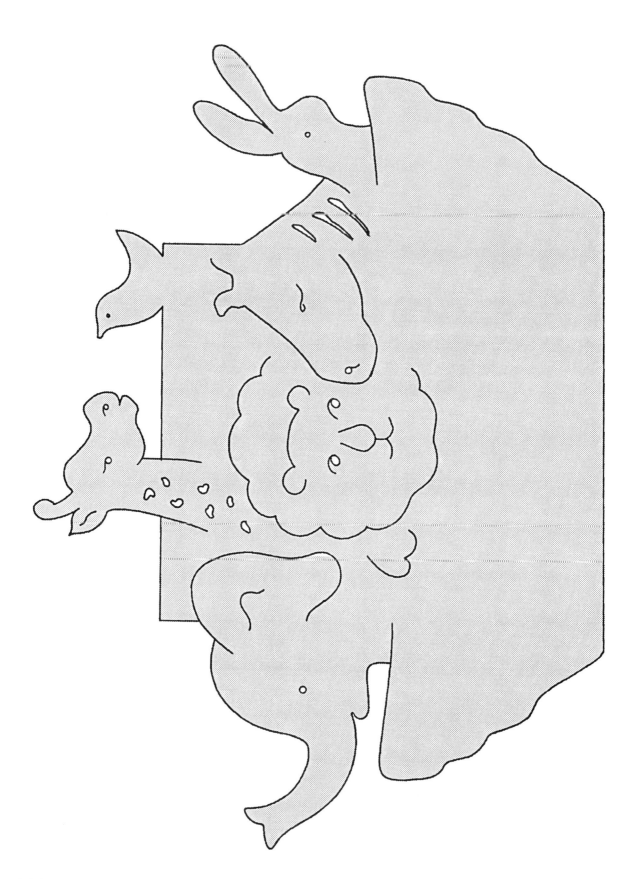

116

Illus. 49. Painted centerpiece candle should be cut from ¾" to 1½"-thick material.

Illus. 50. Nativity scene cut from a piece of ¾"-thick prestained pine (pattern on next page).

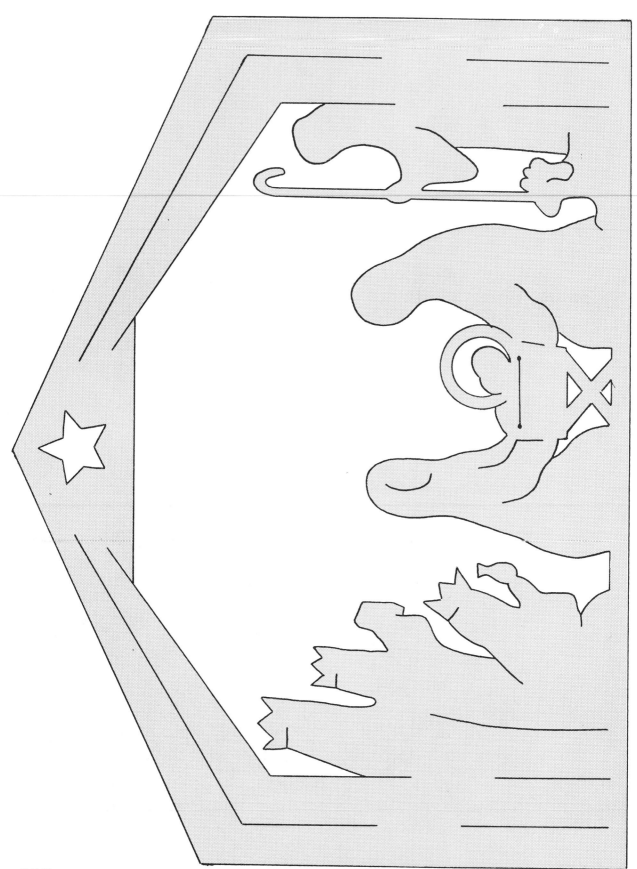

Illus. 51. Christmas shelf with miniature cutouts. Patterns on pages 120 and 121.

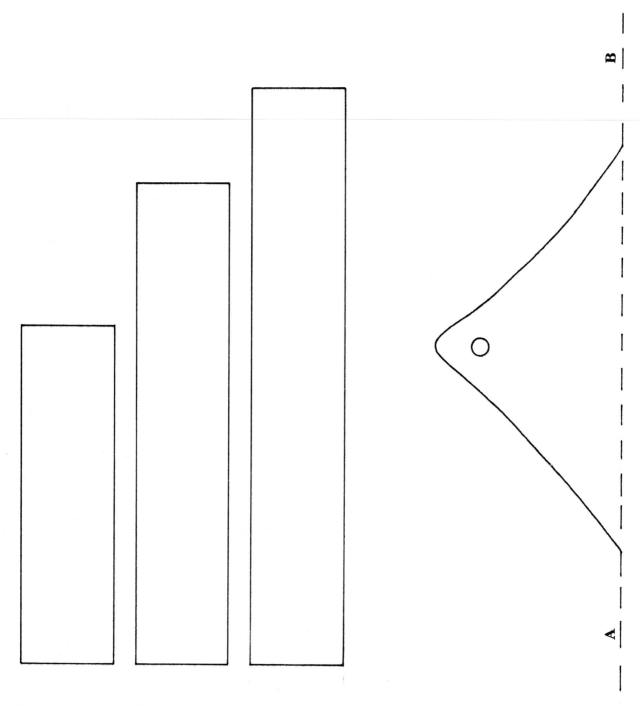

B

A

Rectangles are shelf patterns. Cut them out of
¼-inch stock.

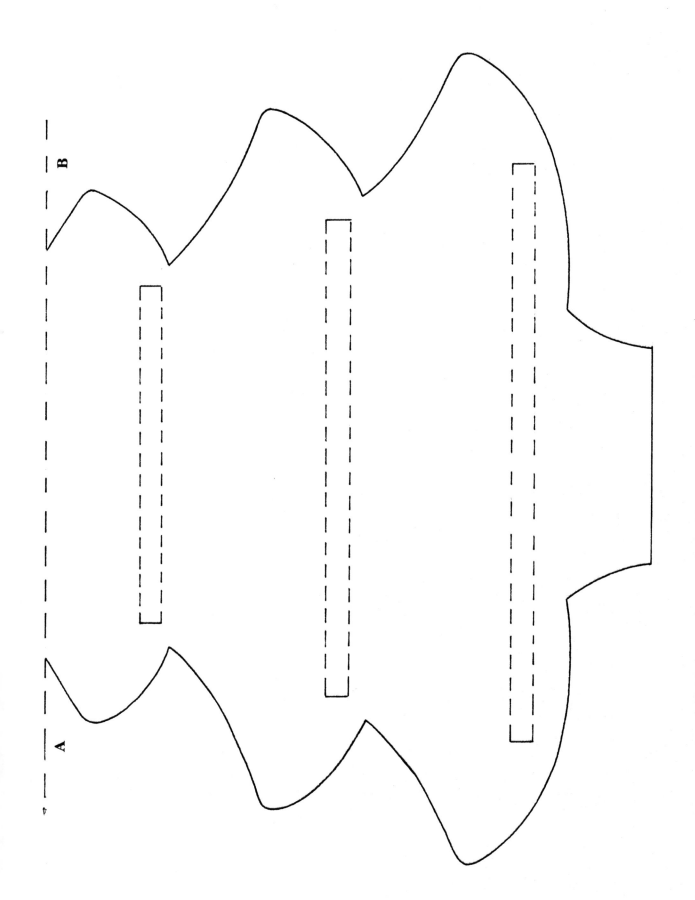

A

B

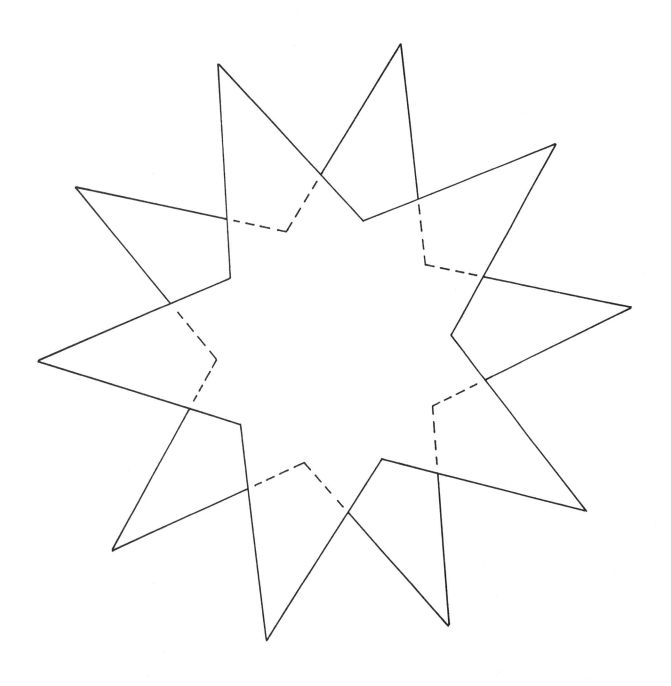

Pages 123 and 124. Two layers are cut separately and glued in place for each star.

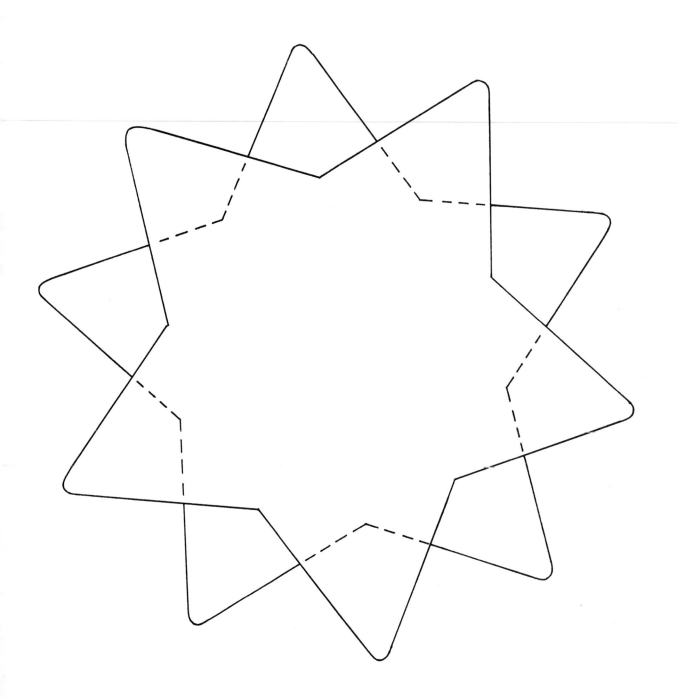

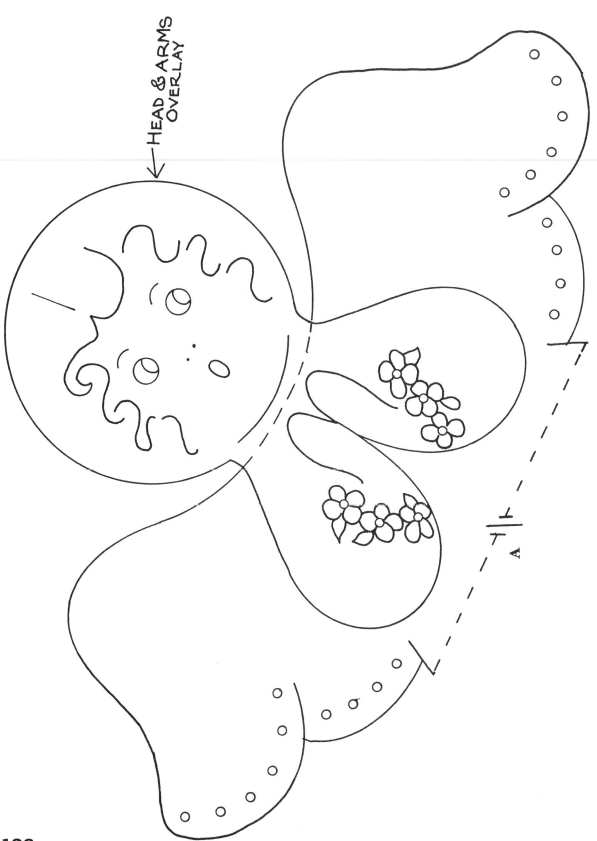

HEAD & ARMS OVERLAY

A

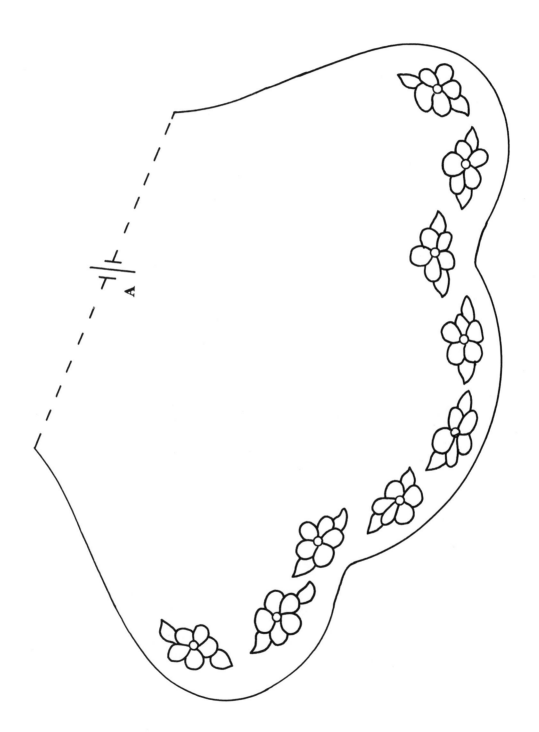

A

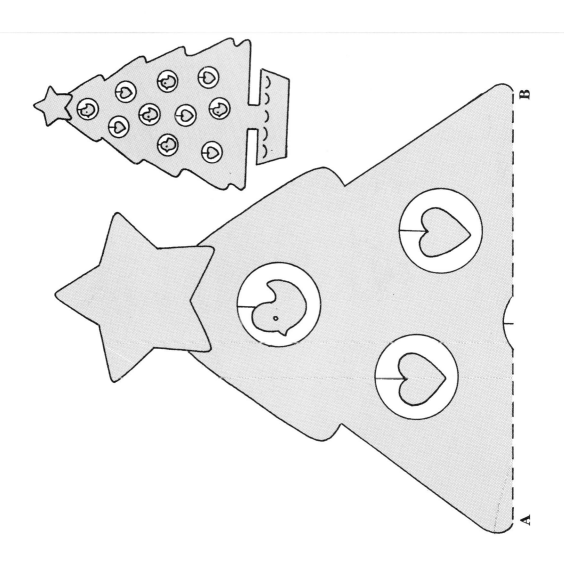

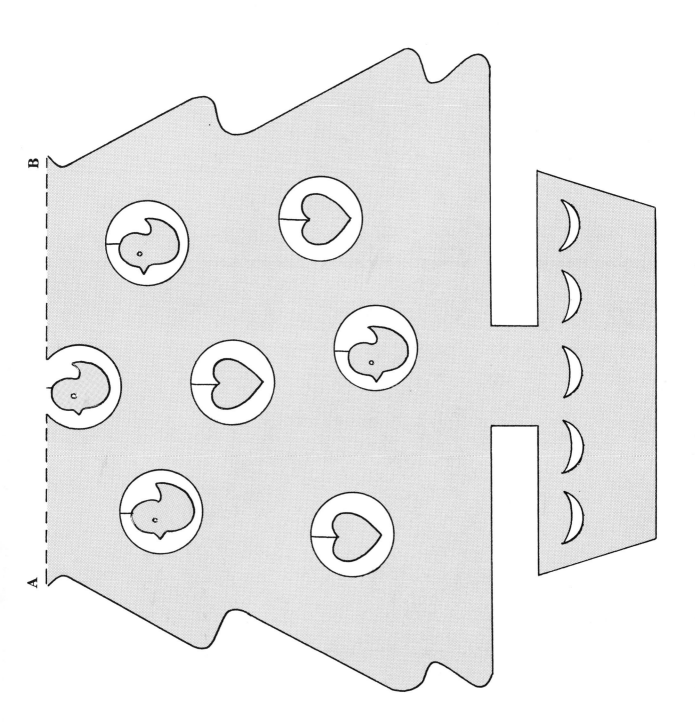

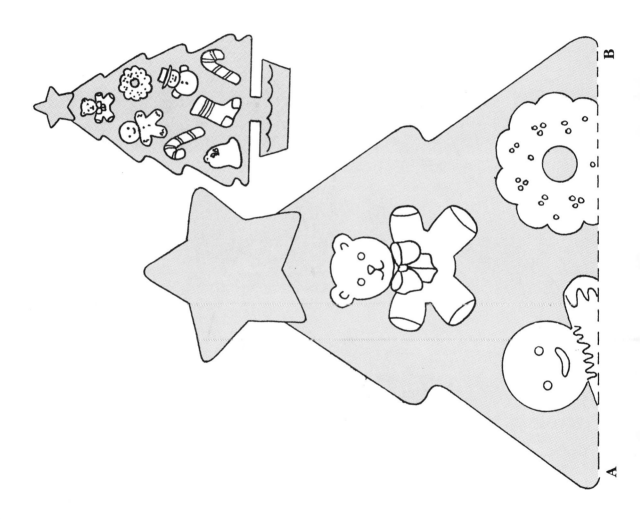

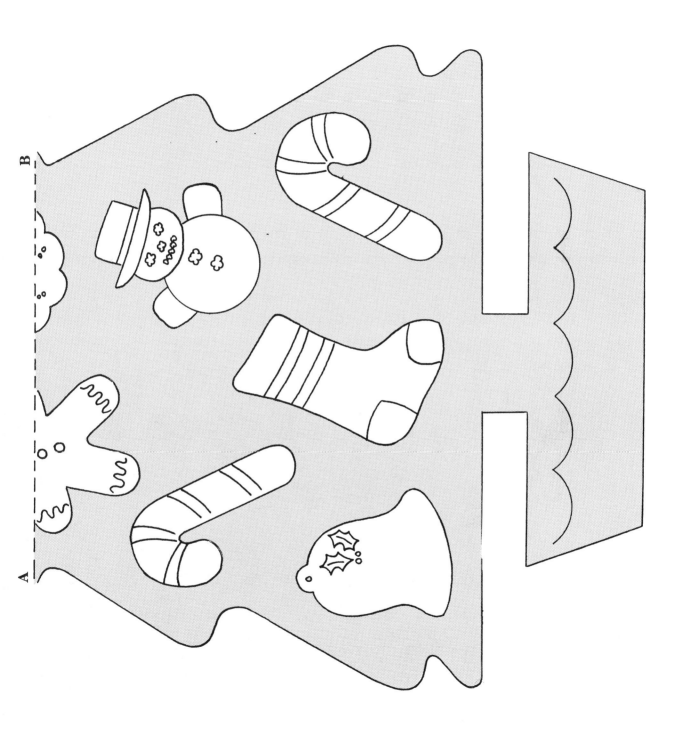

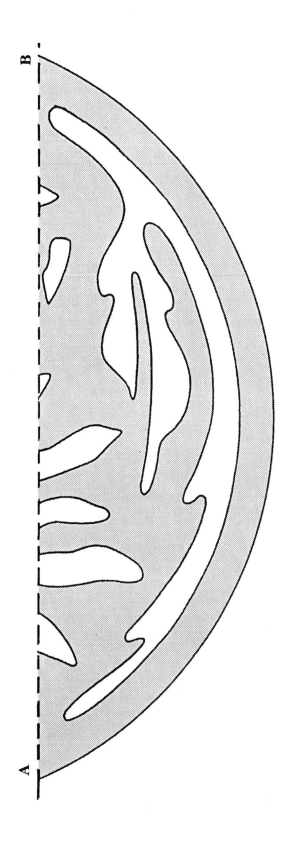

A

B

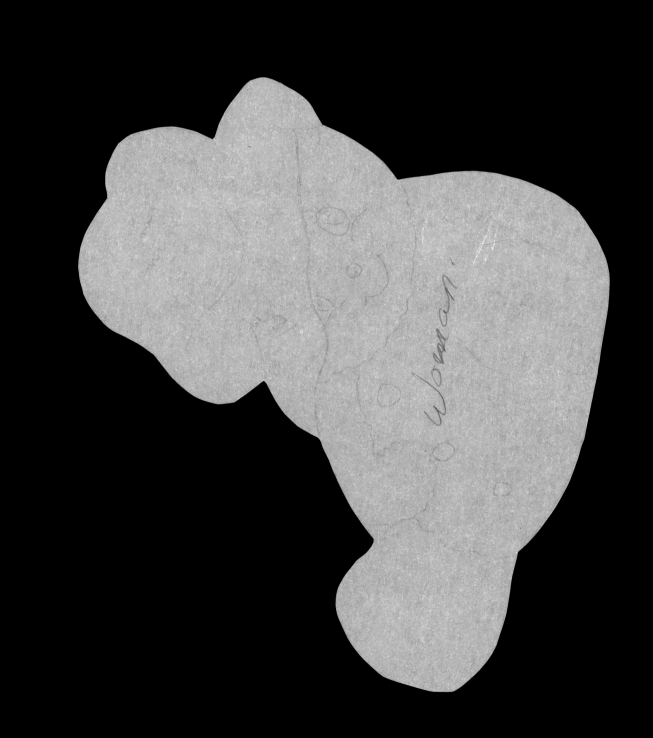

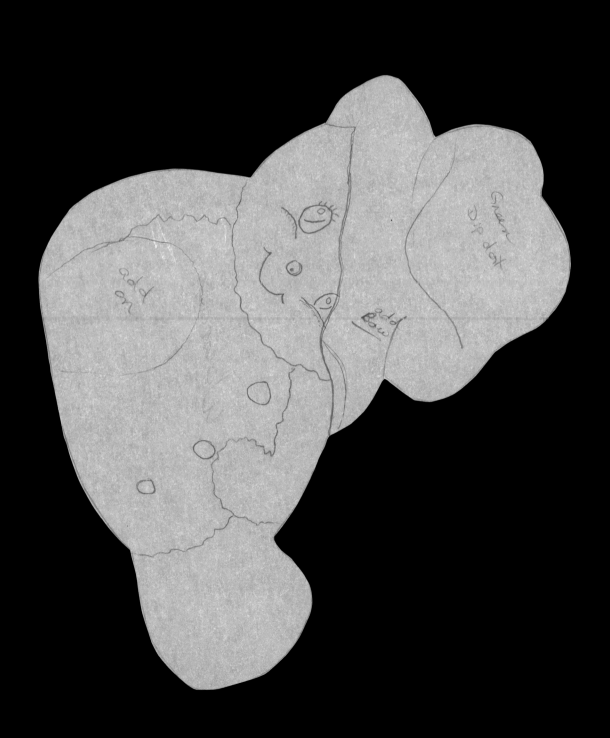

Illus. 52. Trees sawn from thick stock and painted.

139

Illus. 53. Hanging tree with suspended hearts.

Illus. 54. Dimensional tree, designed by Edward Toby, features concentric cuts in ¾"-thick wood or plywood to nest individual parts. Note: Parts are very fragile at short grains when the pattern is made of solid stock.

BASE, $\frac{3}{4}$" THICK

10°

BASE

Illus. 55. A look at the individual pieces of the dimensional tree; when used separately, they also can be decorative.

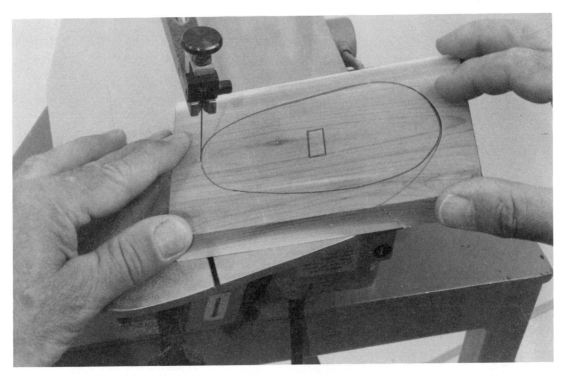

Illus. 56. Bevel-sawing the tree base, with the table adjusted to approximately 10 degrees.

Illus. 57. Cut out letters from ¾"-thick pine. Note: all outside edges may be rounded using a ⅜"-radius corner-rounding bit.

Illus. 58. Rounding the outside edges. A ⅜" corner-rounding bit is used with a special self-made router base of clear plastic with zero clearance around the protruding bit. The routing pad, as shown, permits routing workpieces without clamping.

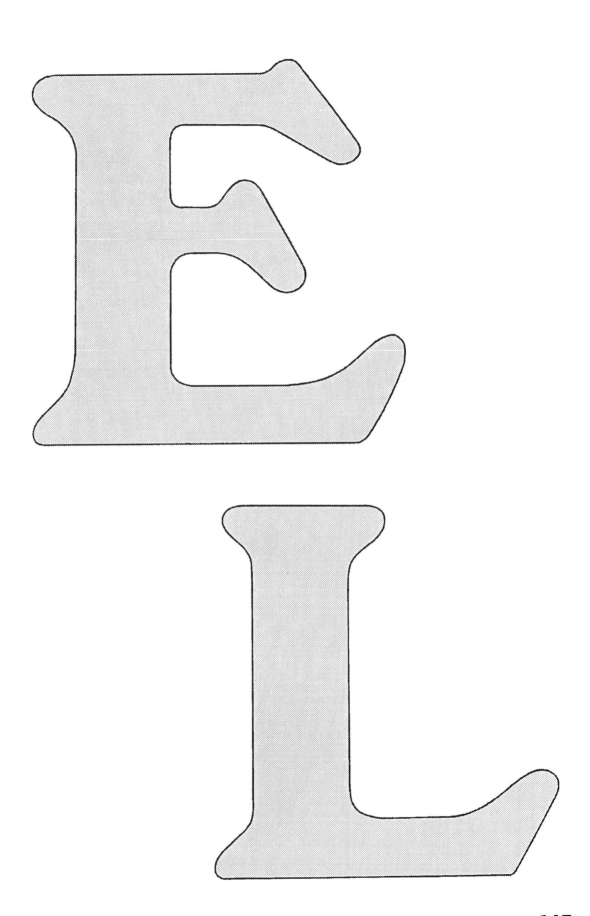

147

Illus. 59. Use the Santa alphabet to spell JOY, as shown, or any other seasonal messages.

Current Books by Patrick Spielman

Carving Wild Animals: Life-Size Wood Figures. Spielman and renowned woodcarver Bill Dehos show how to carve more than 20 magnificent creatures of the North American wild. A cougar, black bear, prairie dog, squirrel, raccoon, and fox are some of the life-size animals included. Step-by-step, photo-filled instructions and multiple-view patterns, plus tips on the use of tools, wood selection, finishing, and polishing, help bring each animal to life. Oversized. Over 300 photos. 16 pages in full color. 240 pages.

Classic Fretwork Scroll Saw Patterns. Spielman and coauthor James Reidle provide over 140 imaginative patterns inspired by and derived from mid- to late-19th-century scroll-saw masters. This book covers nearly 30 categories of patterns and includes a brief review of scroll-saw techniques and how to work with patterns. The patterns include ornamental numbers and letters, beautiful birds, signs, wall pockets, silhouettes, a sleigh, jewelry boxes, toy furniture, and more. 192 pages.

Country Mailboxes. Spielman and co-author Paul Meisel have come up with the 20 best country-style mailbox designs. They include an old pump fire wagon, a Western saddle, a Dalmatian, and even a boy fishing. Simple instructions cover cutting, painting, decorating, and installation. Over 200 illustrations. 4 pages in color. 164 pages.

Gluing & Clamping. A thorough, up-to-date examination of one of the most critical steps in woodworking. Spielman explores the features of every type of glue—from traditional animal-hide glues to the newest epoxies—the clamps and tools needed, the bonding properties of different wood species, safety tips, and all tech-niques from edge-to-edge and end-to-end gluing to applying plastic laminates. Also included is a glossary of terms. Over 500 illustrations. 256 pages.

Making Country-Rustic Wood Projects. Hundreds of photos, patterns, and detailed scaled drawings reveal construction methods, woodworking techniques, and Spielman's professional secrets for making indoor and outdoor furniture in the distinctly attractive Country-Rustic style. Covered are all aspects of furniture making from choosing the best wood for the job to texturing smooth boards. Among the dozens of projects are mailboxes, cabinets, shelves, coffee tables, weather vanes, doors, panelling, plant stands, and many other durable and economical pieces. 400 illustrations. 4 pages in color. 164 pages.

Making Wood Bowls with a Router & Scroll Saw. Using scroll-saw rings, inlays, fretted edges, and much more, Spielman and master craftsman Carl Roehl have developed a completely new approach to creating decorative bowls. Over 200 illustrations. 8 pages in color. 168 pages.

Making Wood Decoys. This clear, step-by-step approach to the basics of decoy carving is abundantly illustrated with close-up photos for designing, selecting, and obtaining woods; tools; feather detailing; painting; and finishing of decorative and working decoys. Six different professional decoy artists are featured. Photo gallery (4 pages in full color) along with numerous detailed plans for various popular decoys. 164 pages.

Making Wood Signs. Designing, selecting woods and tools, and every process through finishing clearly covered. Instructions for hand- and power-carving, routing, and sandblasting techniques for small to huge signs. Foolproof guides for professional letters and ornaments. Hundreds of photos (4 pages in full color). Lists sources for supplies and special tooling. 148 pages.

New Router Handbook. This updated and expanded version of the definitive guide to routing continues to revolutionize router use. The text, with over 1,000 illustrations, covers familiar and new routers, bits, accessories, and tables available today; complete maintenance and safety techniques; a multitude of techniques for both hand-held and mounted routers; plus dozens of helpful shop-made fixtures and jigs. 384 pages.

Original Scroll Saw Shelf Patterns. Patrick Spielman and Loren Raty provide over 50 original, full-size patterns for wall shelves, which may be copied and applied directly to wood. Photographs of finished shelves are included, as well as information on choosing woods, stack sawing, and finishing. 4 pages in color. 132 pages.

Realistic Decoys. Spielman and master carver Keith Bridenhagen reveal their successful techniques for carving, feather texturing, painting, and finishing wood decoys. Details you can't find elsewhere—anatomy, attitudes, markings, and the easy, step-by-step approach to perfect delicate procedures—make this book invaluable. Includes listings for contests, shows, and sources of tools and supplies. 274 close-up photos. 8 pages in color. 232 pages.

Router Basics. With over 200 close-up, step-by-step photos and drawings, this valuable starter handbook will guide the new owner, as well as provide a spark to owners for whom the router isn't the tool they turn to most often. Covers all the basic router styles, along with how-it-works descriptions of all its major features. Includes sections on bits and accessories, as well as square-cutting and trimming, case and furniture routing, cutting circles and arcs, template and freehand routing, and using the router with a router table. 128 pages.

Router Jigs & Techniques. A practical encyclopedia of information, covering the latest equipment to use with the router, it describes all the newest commercial routing machines, along with jigs, bits, and other aids and devices. The book not only provides invaluable tips on how to determine which router and bits to buy, it explains how to get the most out of the equipment once it is bought. Over 800 photos and illustrations. 384 pages.

Scroll Saw Basics. Features more than 275 illustrations covering basic techniques and accessories. Sections include types of saws, features, selection of blades, safety, and how to use patterns. Half a dozen patterns are included to help the scroll saw user get started. Basic cutting techniques are covered, including inside cuts, bevel cuts, stack-sawing, and others. 128 pages.

Scroll Saw Country Patterns. With 300 full-size patterns in 28 categories, this selection of projects covers an extraordinary range, with instructions every step of the way. Projects include farm animals, people, birds, and butterflies, plus letter and key holders, coasters, switch plates, country hearts, and more. Directions for piercing, drilling, sanding, and finishing, as well as tips on using special tools. 4 pages in color. 196 pages.

Scroll Saw Fretwork Patterns. This companion book to *Scroll Saw Fretwork Techniques & Projects* features over 200 fabulous, full-size fretwork patterns. These patterns, drawn by James Reidle, include popular classic designs, plus an array of imaginative contemporary ones. Choose from a variety of numbers, signs, brackets, animals, miniatures, and silhouettes, and more. 256 pages.

Scroll Saw Fretwork Techniques & Projects. A study in the historical development of fretwork, as well as the tools, techniques, materials, and project styles that have evolved over the past 130 years. Every intricate turn and cut is explained, with over 550 step-by-step photos and illustrations. Patterns for all 32 projects are shown in full color. The book also covers some modern scroll-sawing machines as well as state-of-the-art fretwork and fine scroll-sawing techniques. 8 pages in color. 232 pages.

Scroll Saw Handbook. The workshop manual to this versatile tool includes the basics (how scroll saws work, blades to use, etc.) and the advantages and disadvantages of the general types and specific brand-name models on the market. All cutting techniques are detailed, including compound and bevel sawing, making inlays, reliefs, and recesses, cutting metals and other non-woods, and marquetry. There's even a section on transferring patterns to wood. Over 500 illustrations. 256 pages.

Scroll Saw Holiday Patterns. Patrick and Patricia Spielman provide over 100 full-size, shaded patterns for easy cutting, plus full-color photos of projects. Will serve all your holiday pleasures—all year long. Use these holiday patterns to create decorations, centerpieces, mailboxes, and diverse projects to keep or give as gifts. Standard holidays, as well as the four seasons, birthdays, and anniversaries, are represented. 8 pages of color. 168 pages.

Scroll Saw Pattern Book. The original classic pattern book—over 450 patterns for wall plaques, refrigerator magnets, candle holders, pegboards, jewelry, ornaments, shelves, brackets, picture frames, signboards, and many other projects. Beginning and experienced scroll saw users alike will find something to intrigue and challenge them. 256 pages.

Scroll Saw Patterns for the Country Home. Patrick and Patricia Spielman and Sherri Spielman Valitchka produce a wide-ranging collection of over 200 patterns on country themes, including simple cutouts, mobiles, shelves, sculpture, pull toys, door and window toppers, clock holders, photo frames, layered pictures, and more. Over 80 black-and-white photos and 8 pages of color photos help you to visualize the steps involved as well as the finished projects. General instructions in Spielman's clear and concise style are included. 200 pages.

Scroll Saw Puzzle Patterns. 80 full-size patterns for jigsaw puzzles, stand-up puzzles,

and inlay puzzles. With meticulous attention to detail, Patrick and Patricia Spielman provide instructions and step-by-step photos, along with tips on tools and wood selection, for making dinosaurs, camels, hippopotami, alligators—even a family of elephants! Inlay puzzle patterns include basic shapes, numbers, an accurate piece-together map of the United States, and a host of other colorful educational and enjoyable games for children. 8 pages of color. 264 pages.

Scroll Saw Shelf Patterns. Spielman and master scroll saw designer Loren Raty offer full-size patterns for 44 different shelf styles. Designs include wall shelves, corner shelves, and multi-tiered shelves. The patterns work well with ¼-inch hardwood, plywood or any solid wood. Over 150 illustrations. 4 pages in color. 132 pages.

Scroll Saw Silhouette Patterns. With over 120 designs, Spielman and James Reidle provide an extremely diverse collection of intricate silhouette patterns, ranging from Victorian themes to sports to cowboys. They also include mammals, birds, country and nautical designs, as well as dragons, cars, and Christmas themes. Tips, hints, and advice are included along with detailed photos of finished works. 160 pages.

Sharpening Basics. The ultimate handbook that goes well beyond the "basics" to become the major up-to-date reference work features more than 300 detailed illustrations (mostly photos) explaining every facet of tool sharpening. Sections include bench-sharpening tools, sharpening machines, and safety. Chapters cover cleaning tools, and sharpening all sorts of tools, including chisels, plane blades (irons), hand knives, carving tools, turning tools, drill and boring tools, router and shaper tools, jointer and planer knives, drivers and scrapers, and, of course, saws. 128 pages.

Spielman's Original Scroll Saw Patterns. 262 full-size patterns that don't appear elsewhere feature teddy bears, dinosaurs, sports figures, dancers, cowboy cutouts, Christmas ornaments, and dozens more. Fretwork patterns are included for a Viking ship, framed cutouts, wall-hangers, key-chain miniatures, jewelry, and much more. Hundreds of step-by-step photos and drawings show how to turn, repeat, and crop each design for thousands of variations. 4 pages of color. 228 pages.

Victorian Gingerbread: Patterns & Techniques. Authentic pattern designs (many full-size) cover the full range of indoor and outdoor detailing: brackets, corbels, shelves, grilles, spandrels, balusters, running trim, headers, valances, gable ornaments, screen doors, pickets, trellises, and much more. Also included are complete plans for Victorian mailboxes, house numbers, signs, and more. With clear instructions and helpful drawings by James Reidle, the book also provides tips for making gingerbread trim. 8 pages in color. 200 pages.

Victorian Scroll Saw Patterns. Intricate original designs plus classics from the 19th century are presented in full-size, shaded patterns. Instructions are provided with drawings and photos. Projects include alphabets and numbers, silhouettes and designs for shelves, frames, filigree baskets, plant holders, decorative boxes, picture frames, welcome signs, architectural ornaments, and much more. 160 pages.

Working Green Wood with PEG. Covers every process for making beautiful, inexpensive projects from green wood without cracking, splitting, or warping it. Hundreds of clear photos and drawings show every step from obtaining the raw wood through shaping, treating, and finishing PEG-treated projects. 175 unusual project ideas. Lists supply sources. 120 pages.

Index